THE ULTIMATE PRODUCTIVITY PLANNER

A 90-DAY JOURNAL

THE ULTIMATE PRODUCTIVITY PLANNER

to BUILD Effective HABITS

Lisa S. Griffith, CPO®

ROCKRIDGE
PRESS

Interior and Cover Designer: Erin Yeung
Art Producer: Sue Bischofberger
Editor: Nana K. Twumasi
Production Manager: Riley Hoffman
Production Editor: Melissa Edeburn

Author photo courtesy of ©Julie Brigidi, Bristol Workshops in Photography.

ISBN: Print 978-1-64152-670-8

INTRODUCTION

Time is really the only capital any human being has, and the one thing he can't afford to waste.

—THOMAS EDISON

Productivity can be a tricky beast. Feeling productive and actually being productive are not always the same thing. Checking a bunch of items off your to-do list feels great, but if finding time for the things you *want* to do in addition to the things you *need* to do isn't happening, you can be fooled into thinking you're more productive than you actually are.

Getting things done, both the big stuff and the small stuff, is key to living a productive life. However, sometimes we get so caught up in the day-to-day grind of the small stuff—household chores, kids' activities, getting the bills paid, staying on top of the clutter—that we let the bigger things go undone. Whether it's tackling that big project at work, writing your great American novel, or finally undertaking that long-awaited kitchen renovation, having a structured plan will help you move closer to completing your goals. Time is finite. We all get the same 24 hours each day. How you use that time is the key to achieving balance in work and in life.

As a wife, mother of two, and, previously, a teacher, a director, and an administrator of performing arts groups in schools and churches, I spent years just trying to keep my head above water. Forget the whole head— sometimes I would have been happy just keeping one nostril above the surface! Most days were a mad scramble: getting from one activity to the next, frantically trying to get everything done, and falling into bed late at night, only to face the whole circus again the next day.

Sometimes the effort of just *remembering* what I had to do was more than I could manage. I finally realized that I needed to put a master plan into place. Figuring out what I really wanted more time for, and acknowledging what I had to let go of and what was nonnegotiable in my life, required a structured, written plan. That plan involved keeping track of my time for what I *had* to do so I could make time for the things that I *wanted* to do.

The results were life changing. Now, as a productivity and organizing consultant, I use the same structured approach with my clients, and they have found great success and have more time for the things they want to do each day. I hope this planner affords you the same kind of positive change in your life.

Putting a concrete plan into place to manage your time is crucial to maximizing your productivity. Writing down your goals, tracking your time, and establishing your priorities are critical tasks for getting what you need to do out of the way so you have the time for the activities that bring joy to your life. Whether your goal is spending more time with your family, reaching the next rung on the ladder at work, taking better care of yourself physically, having more leisure time for hobbies or volunteer work, or finally being able to take that longed-for vacation, establishing a master plan and putting some structure around it will help you get there.

If you've felt trapped in the hamster wheel of daily life, grinding away at what you have to do and never getting to the things you enjoy, this planner is for you. Know that the power to change your life lies within you. Take some time over the next 90 days to gain control of your schedule, create some new habits, maximize your productivity, and make some space in your life for joy!

GETTING THE MOST FROM THIS PLANNER

At some point, the pain of not doing it becomes greater than the pain of doing it.

—STEVEN PRESSFIELD

The Ultimate Productivity Planner is a tool to boost your productivity over the next three months. Designed for daily use, this planner will help you create and maintain new habits that will last far beyond three months. Because you will be recording information in it every day, you'll want to keep it handy by establishing a "home" where it will live, such as a spot on your desk or kitchen countertop or in your briefcase or purse. When you need to pull it out, you'll always know exactly where to find it!

THE BASICS

Taking time to write down one's goals is proven to help people manage their time more effectively and to increase their productivity. Do you find that your days tend to slip away with few accomplishments, or that you find yourself looking at the clock at the end of each day thinking, "Where the heck did the time go, and what did I get done today?" If so, writing clear goals for your time will help you get things done.

Starting now, you'll be using this planner religiously every day for the next three months to create and reach your goals and learn effective productivity habits. With regular use, this planner will help you become more productive and goal oriented!

Your goals should be S.M.A.R.T.—Specific, Measurable, Achievable, Relevant, and Time-bound:

- **Specific** means your goals should be phrased in simple and clear terms and easily defined, and they should specify exactly what needs to be done.
- **Measurable** means you're able to establish concrete ways to measure progress in attaining your goals and to determine when it is achieved.
- **Achievable** indicates a goal that challenges you but is within the scope of your knowledge, skills, and abilities. You want to have the ability to achieve your goals.
- **Relevant** refers to your goals being worthwhile and appropriate for your stage of life. Ask yourself why each goal is important to you.
- **Time-bound** means you must establish a deadline for accomplishing each step of your goals. Deadlines help create a sense of urgency, and you are more likely to complete goals associated with a timeline.

The key to success in getting more out of your time and increasing your productivity is planning. Spending a small amount of time planning out your day each day, and a slightly bigger chunk of time at the beginning of each week planning out your week, will be critical to your progress. The goal of this planner is to provide you with a tool to make that process simple and straightforward.

Often, I hear busy people lament, "I don't have time to plan!" And my response is always, "You don't have time *not* to plan!" Take just a few minutes every morning or each night to plan the day ahead so that you know exactly what you want to accomplish. At the end of each day, review that day's goals and tasks, and move the incomplete tasks to the next day. Every single day, you get to see yourself move closer to achieving your larger goals.

It's important to establish some planning time before the week begins. Many people find Sunday afternoons or evenings to be a great time to do this task. Look ahead at the week to come, check your calendar for scheduled commitments, pull tasks from your to-do list, and schedule a specific time each day for them to be accomplished. If those tasks from your list aren't written into your calendar, the odds are that they will never get done.

When unexpected obligations interfere with what you had planned to do, it's important to reschedule incomplete tasks at a specific time on another day. In addition, create goals for the entire week, not just daily goals. Planning relieves the "Monday is coming" anxiety that often keeps people from sleeping well on Sunday nights! Instead of dreading Mondays, you'll know exactly how much you'll be getting done and off your plate.

The Ultimate Productivity Planner helps you not only with daily and weekly plans, but also with monthly plans. At the beginning of each month, take some extra planning time to establish goals that can be broken down into weekly and daily tasks. Once you establish the habit of writing down your goals and plans for accomplishing them each day, you will be amazed how much more productive you will be.

WHY 90 DAYS?

Most planners encompass 12 to 18 months, which can be an overwhelming amount of time to try to plan. This planner is designed to help you establish the planning habit. Ninety days is the optimal time period for truly cementing a new habit.

THE FEATURES

As you work with this planner, you will find color-coded pages with space to plan daily, weekly, and monthly goals and the tasks to accomplish them, along with some helpful tips on managing your time more efficiently so you can increase your productivity. You'll find samples of completed planner pages in this book. The sections of the planner are as follows:

- Orange for Monthly planning
- Green for Weekly planning
- Purple for Daily planning
- Red for Monthly review

To make this an even more useful resource, I've also included content to help you on your journey toward effective productivity. You'll find information on popular productivity techniques such as Pomodoro and timeboxing, as well as suggestions for dealing with distractions, avoiding time vampires, and much more.

GOALS FOR THIS MONTH

1. Research contractors for kitchen renovation
2. Submit expense reports
3. Exercise 3 days per week

1	22
2	23
3 Plan upcoming staff meeting	24
4	25 Stay on top of finances.
5	26
6	27
7	28
8	29
9	30
10	31
11	
12 Akilah's birthday	
13	
14	
15	
16	
17	
18	
19	
20	
21	

NOTES AND REMINDERS

Remember gift for Akilah's birthday.

Check website for vacation rentals.

Research computer repair recommendations.

THE WEEK AHEAD

GOALS FOR THIS WEEK

1. Post on social media asking for contractor
2. Collect receipts for expenses
3. Research what exercise classes are available in the area.

MONDAY

Post on Facebook asking friends for contractor referrals

TUESDAY

Pull receipts from car, briefcase/purse

WEDNESDAY

Gather receipts from office desk

THURSDAY

Review YMCA classes.

FRIDAY

Complete and submit expense report.

SATURDAY

Contact 3 contractors for estimates.

SUNDAY

THE PLAN FOR TODAY

TODAY'S GOAL
Balance business checking account.

HIGH-IMPACT TASKS
Send out invoices to clients for services payments due.

TO DO'S
- Record expenses and payments into Quickbooks.
-
-
-
-
-
-

NOTES

THIS MONTH IN REVIEW

1. Did I accomplish my goals for the month?

I called/e-mailed 3 contractors
I filled out and turned in my
expense report on time.

3. If my monthly, weekly, or daily goals were not met, what prevented this?

I procrastinated on researching
options for regular exercise,
because I wasn't sure what I
would enjoy doing.

2. Did doing so get me closer to achieving a long-term goal?

Yes - I have accomplished
the first step in beginning
my kitchen reno

Yes - I will finally be reimbursed
for expenses so I can put the
money toward my vacation

4. How will I solve this problem next month?

I will find out what my friends
are doing for regular exercise and
ask them what they enjoy about
what they do.

| MONTH | May | YEAR | 2020 |

NOTES

....
....
....
....
....
....
....
....
....
....
....
....
....
....
....
....
....
....
....
....
....
....
....
....
....
....
....
....
....
....

WORK LESS, LIVE MORE

Use this planner faithfully for the next three months, and you will achieve solid results. Once you've established the habit of planning out your time with goals in mind, you will find that you spend less time spinning your wheels and feeling stressed, and more time doing the things that bring you joy.

90-DAY PLANNER

THIS MONTH IN FOCUS

GOALS FOR THIS MONTH

....

....

....

1	....	22	....
2	....	23	....
3	....	24	....
4	....	25	....
5	....	26	....
6	....	27	....
7	....	28	....
8	....	29	....
9	....	30	....
10	....	31	....
11	....		
12	....		
13	....		
14	....		
15	....		
16	....		
17	....		
18	....		
19	....		
20	....		
21	....		

NOTES AND REMINDERS

THE WEEK AHEAD

WEEK BEGINNING   /   /

GOALS FOR THIS WEEK

....

....

....

MONDAY

....

TUESDAY

....

WEDNESDAY

....

THURSDAY

....

FRIDAY

....

SATURDAY

....

SUNDAY

....

THE PLAN FOR TODAY

DATE   /   /

TODAY'S GOAL

....
....
....

HIGH-IMPACT TASKS

....
....
....
....
....
....

TO DO'S

- ....
- ....
- ....
- ....
- ....
- ....
- ....

NOTES

....
....
....
....
....

THE PLAN FOR TODAY

TODAY'S GOAL

....
....
....

HIGH-IMPACT TASKS

....
....
....
....
....
....

TO DO'S

- [ ] ....
- [ ] ....
- [ ] ....
- [ ] ....
- [ ] ....
- [ ] ....
- [ ] ....

NOTES

....
....
....
....
....

THE PLAN FOR TODAY

TODAY'S GOAL

....
....
....

HIGH-IMPACT TASKS

....
....
....
....
....
....

TO DO'S

- ....
- ....
- ....
- ....
- ....
- ....
- ....

NOTES

....
....
....
....
....

DEFINING PRODUCTIVITY

According to Dictionary.com, productivity is "the quality, state, or fact of being able to generate, create, enhance, or bring forth goods and services." However, I have found that when asked what they consider "being productive" to mean, most people say it is getting things done. As a productivity consultant, I can tell you it's about far more than simply "bring[ing] forth goods and services." It's about the effective and efficient use of time, effort, energy, and resources in getting the *important* things done. Establishing clear priorities and creating goals based on those priorities is crucial to being effectively productive, rather than just "getting stuff done."

Often, we fritter away a great deal of our valuable time on smaller tasks that may make us feel productive but don't move us toward accomplishing our larger goals in life. Figuring out how to get the small stuff out of the way so that there is time for the important stuff is about prioritizing, decision-making, and time management. There is a common misperception that busy people are getting lots of things done. However, busy doesn't always mean productive. You may be frantically running from task to task but accomplishing very little. Checking things off a to-do list may feel productive, but if your tasks are not moving you forward in your personal or professional life, they are just busywork. If your life is "crazy busy" but you feel as if you're getting nowhere fast, it's time to reevaluate how productive you're really being.

THE PLAN FOR TODAY

DATE / /

TODAY'S GOAL

....
....
....

HIGH-IMPACT TASKS

....
....
....
....
....
....

TO DO'S

- [ ] ....
- [ ] ....
- [ ] ....
- [ ] ....
- [ ] ....
- [ ] ....
- [ ] ....

NOTES

....
....
....
....
....

THE PLAN FOR TODAY

TODAY'S GOAL

....
....
....

HIGH-IMPACT TASKS

....
....
....
....
....
....

TO DO'S

- ....
- ....
- ....
- ....
- ....
- ....
- ....

NOTES

....
....
....
....
....

THE PLAN FOR TODAY

DATE / /

TODAY'S GOAL

....
....
....

HIGH-IMPACT TASKS

....
....
....
....
....
....

TO DO'S

- ☐ ....
- ☐ ....
- ☐ ....
- ☐ ....
- ☐ ....
- ☐ ....
- ☐ ....

NOTES

....
....
....
....
....

THE PLAN FOR TODAY

DATE   /   /

TODAY'S GOAL

....

....

....

HIGH-IMPACT TASKS

....

....

....

....

....

TO DO'S

- ....
- ....
- ....
- ....
- ....
- ....
- ....

NOTES

....

....

....

....

....

We are a culture of people who've bought into the idea that if we stay busy enough, the truth of our lives won't catch up with us.

—BRENÉ BROWN

THE WEEK AHEAD

WEEK BEGINNING   /   /

GOALS FOR THIS WEEK

....

....

....

MONDAY

....

TUESDAY

....

WEDNESDAY

....

THURSDAY

....

FRIDAY

....

SATURDAY

....

SUNDAY

....

THE PLAN FOR TODAY

TODAY'S GOAL

....

....

....

HIGH-IMPACT TASKS

....

....

....

....

....

....

TO DO'S

- ....
- ....
- ....
- ....
- ....
- ....
- ....

NOTES

....

....

....

....

....

THE PLAN FOR TODAY

DATE   /   /

TODAY'S GOAL

....
....
....

HIGH-IMPACT TASKS

....
....
....
....
....
....

TO DO'S

- ....
- ....
- ....
- ....
- ....
- ....
- ....

NOTES

....
....
....
....
....

THE PLAN FOR TODAY

TODAY'S GOAL

....

....

....

HIGH-IMPACT TASKS

....

....

....

....

....

....

TO DO'S

- [ ] ....
- [ ] ....
- [ ] ....
- [ ] ....
- [ ] ....
- [ ] ....
- [ ] ....

NOTES

....

....

....

....

....

THE PLAN FOR TODAY

DATE / /

TODAY'S GOAL

....
....
....

HIGH-IMPACT TASKS

....
....
....
....
....
....

TO DO'S

- ....
- ....
- ....
- ....
- ....
- ....
- ....

NOTES

....
....
....
....
....

MULTITASKING: MYTH OR MAGIC?

When you try to do multiple things at once, you may think you're accomplishing twice as much in the same amount of time you'd normally spend on just one task. In fact, multitasking actually wastes more time than it saves. Instead of doing one thing well and moving on, we do two or more things halfway or poorly and take more time doing each.

The key to productivity is focus. When we try to work on a project while doing other things, we never get into full concentration mode. Your brain really can't fully focus on two things at once. What actually happens is that your brain takes time and energy every time you switch back and forth between tasks. According to research published by the American Psychological Association (2006), these brief seconds can cost you as much as 40 percent of your productive time. A study at Stanford University (Gorlick 2009) found that heavy multitaskers lack attentiveness, struggle with short-term memory, and take longer to complete things than light multitaskers.

Tips for focusing:

- Block out specific time in your day to work on one chosen task.
- Turn off your phone and silence notifications on your computer.
- Commit to working on that one task until it's done or until your time block is over. If the task is not complete, move it forward in your calendar.
- Set aside designated times of the day to read and answer e-mails.
- Work in a place where you're comfortable but not so comfortable that you can't maintain the "work" mind-set. Some people will have no problem working in a relaxation spot, like a bed or couch; others may need a table or desk.

By allowing yourself to fully concentrate on one thing at a time, you will make fewer mistakes, produce work of higher quality, and save time.

THE PLAN FOR TODAY

TODAY'S GOAL

....
....
....

HIGH-IMPACT TASKS

....
....
....
....
....
....

TO DO'S

- ....
- ....
- ....
- ....
- ....
- ....
- ....

NOTES

....
....
....
....
....

THE PLAN FOR TODAY

DATE / /

TODAY'S GOAL

....

....

....

HIGH-IMPACT TASKS

....

....

....

....

....

....

TO DO'S

- ....
- ....
- ....
- ....
- ....
- ....
- ....

NOTES

....

....

....

....

....

THE PLAN FOR TODAY

DATE   /   /

TODAY'S GOAL

....
....
....

HIGH-IMPACT TASKS

....
....
....
....
....
....

TO DO'S

- ....
- ....
- ....
- ....
- ....
- ....
- ....

NOTES

....
....
....
....
....

THE WEEK AHEAD

WEEK BEGINNING   /   /

GOALS FOR THIS WEEK

....
....
....

MONDAY

....

TUESDAY

....

WEDNESDAY

....

THURSDAY

....

FRIDAY

....

SATURDAY

....

SUNDAY

....

THE PLAN FOR TODAY

TODAY'S GOAL

....

....

....

HIGH-IMPACT TASKS

....

....

....

....

....

....

TO DO'S

- ....
- ....
- ....
- ....
- ....
- ....
- ....

NOTES

....

....

....

....

....

THE PLAN FOR TODAY

TODAY'S GOAL

....

....

....

HIGH-IMPACT TASKS

....

....

....

....

....

....

TO DO'S

- [ ] ....
- [ ] ....
- [ ] ....
- [ ] ....
- [ ] ....
- [ ] ....
- [ ] ....

NOTES

....

....

....

....

....

THE PLAN FOR TODAY

TODAY'S GOAL

....
....
....

HIGH-IMPACT TASKS

....
....
....
....
....
....

TO DO'S

- ....
- ....
- ....
- ....
- ....
- ....
- ....

NOTES

....
....
....
....
....

DIVIDE AND CONQUER

Does your to-do list contain a task such as "renovate bathroom"? You may not realize the difference between individual tasks and larger projects.

A *task* can be accomplished in a single step. A *project* is something that requires multiple tasks. When you have a project, break it down into tasks, as in this example:

1. Ask for general contractor recommendations.
2. Check out contractors; see reviews and their previous work.
3. Meet with each contractor and get quotes.
4. Sign a contract with the right contractor and pay a deposit.
5. Begin bathroom renovation.

Taking a few minutes to identify the necessary tasks will save time and diminish angst that could prevent you from starting the project. Once you get the tasks out of your head and into writing, the project will seem less intimidating and more doable.

Once you know the individual tasks, assign each one some time on your calendar. Set a realistic deadline for each task. You'll have a much better idea of how long it will take to complete your project. You also have the satisfaction of checking each step off your list as you accomplish it.

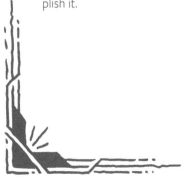

THE PLAN FOR TODAY

DATE   /   /

TODAY'S GOAL

....
....
....

HIGH-IMPACT TASKS

....
....
....
....
....
....

TO DO'S

- [ ] ....
- [ ] ....
- [ ] ....
- [ ] ....
- [ ] ....
- [ ] ....
- [ ] ....

NOTES

....
....
....
....
....

THE PLAN FOR TODAY

TODAY'S GOAL

....
....
....

HIGH-IMPACT TASKS

....
....
....
....
....
....

TO DO'S

- ....
- ....
- ....
- ....
- ....
- ....
- ....

NOTES

....
....
....
....
....

THE PLAN FOR TODAY

DATE   /   /

TODAY'S GOAL

....
....
....

HIGH-IMPACT TASKS

....
....
....
....
....
....

TO DO'S

- ....
- ....
- ....
- ....
- ....
- ....
- ....

NOTES

....
....
....
....
....

THE PLAN FOR TODAY

DATE / /

TODAY'S GOAL

....

....

....

HIGH-IMPACT TASKS

....

....

....

....

....

....

TO DO'S

- ....
- ....
- ....
- ....
- ....
- ....
- ....

NOTES

....

....

....

....

....

THE WEEK AHEAD

WEEK BEGINNING   /   /

GOALS FOR THIS WEEK

....
....
....

MONDAY
....

TUESDAY
....

WEDNESDAY
....

THURSDAY
....

FRIDAY
....

SATURDAY
....

SUNDAY
....

THE PLAN FOR TODAY

TODAY'S GOAL

....
....
....

HIGH-IMPACT TASKS

....
....
....
....
....
....

TO DO'S

- ....
- ....
- ....
- ....
- ....
- ....
- ....

NOTES

....
....
....
....
....

THE PLAN FOR TODAY

DATE / /

TODAY'S GOAL

....
....
....

HIGH-IMPACT TASKS

....
....
....
....
....
....

TO DO'S

- ....
- ....
- ....
- ....
- ....
- ....
- ....

NOTES

....
....
....
....
....

THE PLAN FOR TODAY

DATE   /   /

TODAY'S GOAL

....

....

....

HIGH-IMPACT TASKS

....

....

....

....

....

....

TO DO'S

- ....
- ....
- ....
- ....
- ....
- ....
- ....

NOTES

....

....

....

....

....

THE PLAN FOR TODAY

DATE / /

TODAY'S GOAL

....

....

....

HIGH-IMPACT TASKS

....

....

....

....

....

....

TO DO'S

- [ ] ....
- [ ] ....
- [ ] ....
- [ ] ....
- [ ] ....
- [ ] ....
- [ ] ....

NOTES

....

....

....

....

....

THE FIVE-MINUTE RULE

The five-minute rule can help you clear away the smaller stuff that quickly accumulates. It's a simple rule: If you can get the task done in five or fewer minutes, do it right away.

For example, when the mail arrives each day or you sit down at your desk, take the time to deal with any task that can be finished within five minutes. Make that quick phone call or send that short e-mail. If you can get it accomplished within five minutes, just do it on the spot. You'll be surprised how easily this keeps the little stuff on your to-do list from blossoming out of control, and it gets these tasks out of the way.

The five-minute rule also comes in handy when you find yourself with a little bit of extra time in between commitments or when you're on endless hold on the phone. Having a list of quick, easy five-minute tasks to do before you go out or while you wait helps make time later for more time-consuming tasks that require concentrated focus.

One caveat to this rule: If you habitually run late because you're always trying to do "one more thing," be realistic about how much time you really have and choose just one quick task, rather than three or four. Remember, everyone's time is important, and you don't want to make others feel bad or as if you don't care about their time by being consistently late. A large part of getting organized and scheduling tasks is learning to effectively manage your time, taking ownership, and being accountable for your ability to get things done. Acknowledging that others may view time differently than you do is a crucial step in managing your time better.

THE PLAN FOR TODAY

DATE / /

TODAY'S GOAL

....
....
....

HIGH-IMPACT TASKS

....
....
....
....
....
....

TO DO'S

- ....
- ....
- ....
- ....
- ....
- ....
- ....

NOTES

....
....
....
....
....

THE PLAN FOR TODAY

DATE / /

TODAY'S GOAL

....
....
....

HIGH-IMPACT TASKS

....
....
....
....
....
....

TO DO'S

- ....
- ....
- ....
- ....
- ....
- ....
- ....

NOTES

....
....
....
....
....

THE PLAN FOR TODAY

TODAY'S GOAL

....
....
....

HIGH-IMPACT TASKS

....
....
....
....
....
....

TO DO'S

- [ ] ....
- [ ] ....
- [ ] ....
- [ ] ....
- [ ] ....
- [ ] ....
- [ ] ....

NOTES

....
....
....
....
....

Out of clutter, find simplicity. From discord, find harmony. In the middle of difficulty lies opportunity.

—ALBERT EINSTEIN

THE WEEK AHEAD

GOALS FOR THIS WEEK

....

....

....

MONDAY

....

TUESDAY

....

WEDNESDAY

....

THURSDAY

....

FRIDAY

....

SATURDAY

....

SUNDAY

....

THE PLAN FOR TODAY

DATE   /   /

TODAY'S GOAL

....
....
....

HIGH-IMPACT TASKS

....
....
....
....
....
....

TO DO'S

- ....
- ....
- ....
- ....
- ....
- ....
- ....

NOTES

....
....
....
....
....

THE PLAN FOR TODAY

DATE   /   /

TODAY'S GOAL

....
....
....

HIGH-IMPACT TASKS

....
....
....
....
....
....

TO DO'S

- ....
- ....
- ....
- ....
- ....
- ....
- ....

NOTES

....
....
....
....
....

THE PLAN FOR TODAY

DATE / /

TODAY'S GOAL

....
....
....

HIGH-IMPACT TASKS

....
....
....
....
....
....

TO DO'S

- ....
- ....
- ....
- ....
- ....
- ....
- ....

NOTES

....
....
....
....
....

DISORGANIZED SPACE = LOST PRODUCTIVITY

Your physical space affects how much you get done. If your space is disorganized and cluttered, you are losing precious time every day dealing with the mess. An article in *Psychology Today* (Carter 2012) explains how a messy or cluttered space visually distracts you, makes you anxious, and causes your brain stress. All your brain sees are piles, and it thinks, "Will I ever be finished?" Then it's a short leap to "If I can't ever finish, why bother trying?"

Research from Princeton University (Doland 2011) indicates that clutter affects our ability to focus and can make it harder to process information. Getting organized takes time, but it doesn't have to be painful! Many people find decluttering satisfying, and nothing beats a fresh, clean work space.

Tips for decluttering:

- Sort through the paperwork on your desk, kitchen counter, and dining room table.
- Decide what paperwork to keep and what to toss.
  - Anything out of date, duplicated, or irrelevant can be discarded or shredded.
  - Important papers can be either digitized or stored.
  - Check to see if work papers are already digitized, and either toss or store them.
- Get the paperwork you keep into an organized filing system.
- Clear out your closet and keep only the clothing that fits you and makes you feel good.
  - Donate your items to a local charity or shelter. Get a receipt, because donations are tax deductible!
- Take everything off your desk and wipe down the desktop. It feels great to sit down at a clean space.

Having a clean space frees your time and your mind for more important things and reduces the stress of dealing with all that clutter.

THE PLAN FOR TODAY

DATE   /   /

TODAY'S GOAL

....
....
....

HIGH-IMPACT TASKS

....
....
....
....
....
....

TO DO'S

- ....
- ....
- ....
- ....
- ....
- ....
- ....

NOTES

....
....
....
....
....

THE PLAN FOR TODAY

DATE   /   /

TODAY'S GOAL

....
....
....

HIGH-IMPACT TASKS

....
....
....
....
....
....

TO DO'S

- ....
- ....
- ....
- ....
- ....
- ....
- ....

NOTES

....
....
....
....
....

THE PLAN FOR TODAY

DATE / /

TODAY'S GOAL

....
....
....

HIGH-IMPACT TASKS

....
....
....
....
....
....

TO DO'S

- ....
- ....
- ....
- ....
- ....
- ....
- ....

NOTES

....
....
....
....
....

THE PLAN FOR TODAY

TODAY'S GOAL

....
....
....

HIGH-IMPACT TASKS

....
....
....
....
....
....

TO DO'S

- ....
- ....
- ....
- ....
- ....
- ....
- ....

NOTES

....
....
....
....
....

The beginning is half of every action.

—DAVID ALLEN

THIS MONTH IN REVIEW

1. Did I accomplish my goals for the month?

....
....
....
....
....
....
....
....

3. If my monthly, weekly, or daily goals were not met, what prevented this?

....
....
....
....
....
....
....

2. Did doing so get me closer to achieving a long-term goal?

....
....
....
....
....
....
....
....

4. How will I solve this problem next month?

....
....
....
....
....
....
....
....

MONTH

YEAR

NOTES

THIS MONTH IN FOCUS

GOALS FOR THIS MONTH

....

....

....

1	....	22	....
2	....	23	....
3	....	24	....
4	....	25	....
5	....	26	....
6	....	27	....
7	....	28	....
8	....	29	....
9	....	30	....
10	....	31	....
11	....		
12	....		
13	....		
14	....		
15	....		
16	....		
17	....		
18	....		
19	....		
20	....		
21	....		

NOTES AND REMINDERS

THE WEEK AHEAD

WEEK BEGINNING   /   /

GOALS FOR THIS WEEK

....

....

....

MONDAY

....

TUESDAY

....

WEDNESDAY

....

THURSDAY

....

FRIDAY

....

SATURDAY

....

SUNDAY

....

THE PLAN FOR TODAY

DATE   /   /

TODAY'S GOAL

....
....
....

HIGH-IMPACT TASKS

....
....
....
....
....
....

TO DO'S

- ....
- ....
- ....
- ....
- ....
- ....
- ....

NOTES

....
....
....
....
....

THE PLAN FOR TODAY

TODAY'S GOAL

....
....
....

HIGH-IMPACT TASKS

....
....
....
....
....
....

TO DO'S

- ....
- ....
- ....
- ....
- ....
- ....
- ....

NOTES

....
....
....
....
....

THE PLAN FOR TODAY

TODAY'S GOAL

....
....
....

HIGH-IMPACT TASKS

....
....
....
....
....
....

TO DO'S

- ....
- ....
- ....
- ....
- ....
- ....
- ....

NOTES

....
....
....
....
....

TIME YOUR APPROACH

Whenever I have a hard time getting started on a project, I set a timer for 15 minutes. Then, I give intense focus to the project until the timer goes off. I can do anything for 15 minutes, even if it's something I dislike. When the timer goes off, I can take a break, work on something else for a while, or quit for the day. Often, getting started is the hardest part, so when the timer goes off, I just keep going.

Research from the University of Illinois at Urbana-Champaign (2011) has shown that the human brain works best in short spurts with frequent breaks. In fact, that research shows that attempting to concentrate on a single task for lengthy periods of time can be counterproductive. The Pomodoro Technique is a time management method that advocates for working in short intervals and then taking a break. This technique recommends intervals of 25 minutes, but you should find the amount of time that works best for you. This method can help you get started. If you put in enough short, concentrated segments of work, over time your project will get done!

The Pomodoro Technique is the opposite of the five-minute rule. With Pomodoro, you are training your brain to focus hard for a limited amount of time, more often to complete larger or longer tasks. Both methods, though, help you create and maintain strong productivity habits. This technique can be most helpful when you notice that you aren't as focused as you need to be.

THE PLAN FOR TODAY

TODAY'S GOAL

....
....
....

HIGH-IMPACT TASKS

....
....
....
....
....
....

TO DO'S

- ....
- ....
- ....
- ....
- ....
- ....
- ....

NOTES

....
....
....
....
....

THE PLAN FOR TODAY

DATE / /

TODAY'S GOAL

....
....
....

HIGH-IMPACT TASKS

....
....
....
....
....
....

TO DO'S

- ....
- ....
- ....
- ....
- ....
- ....
- ....

NOTES

....
....
....
....
....

THE PLAN FOR TODAY

DATE   /   /

TODAY'S GOAL

....

....

....

HIGH-IMPACT TASKS

....

....

....

....

....

....

TO DO'S

- ....
- ....
- ....
- ....
- ....
- ....
- ....

NOTES

....

....

....

....

....

THE PLAN FOR TODAY

TODAY'S GOAL

....
....
....

HIGH-IMPACT TASKS

....
....
....
....
....
....

TO DO'S

- ....
- ....
- ....
- ....
- ....
- ....
- ....

NOTES

....
....
....
....
....

Start by doing what's necessary; then do what's possible; and suddenly you are doing the impossible.

—ST. FRANCIS OF ASSISI

THE WEEK AHEAD

GOALS FOR THIS WEEK

....

....

....

MONDAY

....

TUESDAY

....

WEDNESDAY

....

THURSDAY

....

FRIDAY

....

SATURDAY

....

SUNDAY

....

THE PLAN FOR TODAY

DATE / /

TODAY'S GOAL

....

....

....

HIGH-IMPACT TASKS

....

....

....

....

....

....

TO DO'S

- ....
- ....
- ....
- ....
- ....
- ....
- ....

NOTES

....

....

....

....

....

THE PLAN FOR TODAY

DATE / /

TODAY'S GOAL

....
....
....

HIGH-IMPACT TASKS

....
....
....
....
....
....

TO DO'S

- ....
- ....
- ....
- ....
- ....
- ....
- ....

NOTES

....
....
....
....
....

THE PLAN FOR TODAY

DATE / /

TODAY'S GOAL

....

....

....

HIGH-IMPACT TASKS

....

....

....

....

....

....

TO DO'S

- ....
- ....
- ....
- ....
- ....
- ....
- ....

NOTES

....

....

....

....

....

THE PLAN FOR TODAY

DATE   /   /

TODAY'S GOAL

....
....
....

HIGH-IMPACT TASKS

....
....
....
....
....
....

TO DO'S

- ....
- ....
- ....
- ....
- ....
- ....
- ....

NOTES

....
....
....
....
....

PUSHING PAST PROCRASTINATION

Avoiding difficult things is a common human behavior. Although procrastination feels good in the moment, putting off doing necessary tasks for too long creates stress and affects the quality of your work when you inevitably feel rushed to complete it.

For years, researchers have been trying to pinpoint why chronic procrastinators behave the way they do. Theories abound: Fear of failure, poor time management, difficulty regulating emotions, and executive function disorder are all on the list. Some neuroscientists have theorized that some people prefer others to believe they are lazy instead of incompetent. Whatever the reason for your own procrastination, it's important to get to the root of it. It could be any of the reasons just mentioned or something unique to you. It could be a chronic issue or a situational one.

When my clients struggle to get going on a project, I recommend a great trick to get them started. Brian Tracy (author of *Time Power* and *Eat That Frog!*) calls this tip "eating the biggest, ugliest frog first." Every project or to-do list has a specific component that is the most difficult. When you face a combination of difficult and easier tasks in a project, get the more difficult ones out of the way first. This is called "eating the frog." Do the toughest thing right away. This allows the floodgates of productivity to be open for the rest of your day. Life is full of challenges, and procrastinating only postpones the inevitable. Getting started is often the hardest part, but once you do, the rewards are great. Imagine yourself done, reaping the benefits of more time, more space, or more peace of mind.

THE PLAN FOR TODAY

TODAY'S GOAL

....
....
....

HIGH-IMPACT TASKS

....
....
....
....
....
....

TO DO'S

- ....
- ....
- ....
- ....
- ....
- ....
- ....

NOTES

....
....
....
....
....

THE PLAN FOR TODAY

DATE   /   /

TODAY'S GOAL

....
....
....

HIGH-IMPACT TASKS

....
....
....
....
....
....

TO DO'S

- ....
- ....
- ....
- ....
- ....
- ....
- ....

NOTES

....
....
....
....
....

THE PLAN FOR TODAY

TODAY'S GOAL

....
....
....

HIGH-IMPACT TASKS

....
....
....
....
....
....

TO DO'S

- ....
- ....
- ....
- ....
- ....
- ....
- ....

NOTES

....
....
....
....
....

THE WEEK AHEAD

GOALS FOR THIS WEEK

....

....

....

MONDAY

....

TUESDAY

....

WEDNESDAY

....

THURSDAY

....

FRIDAY

....

SATURDAY

....

SUNDAY

....

THE PLAN FOR TODAY

TODAY'S GOAL

....
....
....

HIGH-IMPACT TASKS

....
....
....
....
....
....

TO DO'S

- ....
- ....
- ....
- ....
- ....
- ....
- ....

NOTES

....
....
....
....
....

THE PLAN FOR TODAY

TODAY'S GOAL

....
....
....

HIGH-IMPACT TASKS

....
....
....
....
....
....

TO DO'S

- ....
- ....
- ....
- ....
- ....
- ....
- ....

NOTES

....
....
....
....
....

THE PLAN FOR TODAY

DATE   /   /

TODAY'S GOAL

....

....

....

HIGH-IMPACT TASKS

....

....

....

....

....

....

TO DO'S

- ....
- ....
- ....
- ....
- ....
- ....
- ....

NOTES

....

....

....

....

....

AVOID TIME VAMPIRES

The *Urban Dictionary* defines a time vampire as "something or someone who literally sucks your time like a vampire sucks blood." Time vampires can be human or inanimate. The human ones usually specialize in interruptions, like the folks who stick their head in your office to say, "Hey, I've got a quick question," or the office gossip who derails your trip to the coffee machine. The best solution to stopping these serial interrupters is learning how to say "no," which is a sometimes uncomfortable, but always necessary, acquired skill.

Saying "no" can often make us feel awkward or uncomfortable, but if you need time to work, take that time, and don't feel bad about it. You are the only one who will protect your time.

If it's your boss interrupting (Davidson 2012), ask what she or he wants you to do first and request clarification of your priorities. Don't be afraid to say, "I am still working on ABC right now, but it should be done by Tuesday. I can start working on XYZ on Tuesday, unless it is a higher priority." This allows both of you to understand the priorities while still protecting your time.

What if you're in charge? Sometimes saying no requires tact and diplomacy. Acknowledge the interrupter's request and try saying, "I understand this is important to you; I am busy right now, but I would very much like to address your question. Can we set up a time to talk later?" Establishing specific times to respond to interruptions helps your staff understand that their needs are being met and that you are setting aside uninterrupted, concentrated time to work on your prioritized goals. This is the key to getting more done.

THE PLAN FOR TODAY

DATE / /

TODAY'S GOAL

....
....
....

HIGH-IMPACT TASKS

....
....
....
....
....
....

TO DO'S

- [ ] ....
- [ ] ....
- [ ] ....
- [ ] ....
- [ ] ....
- [ ] ....
- [ ] ....

NOTES

....
....
....
....
....

THE PLAN FOR TODAY

DATE   /   /

TODAY'S GOAL

....
....
....

HIGH-IMPACT TASKS

....
....
....
....
....
....

TO DO'S

- ....
- ....
- ....
- ....
- ....
- ....
- ....

NOTES

....
....
....
....
....

THE PLAN FOR TODAY

DATE / /

TODAY'S GOAL

....
....
....

HIGH-IMPACT TASKS

....
....
....
....
....
....

TO DO'S

- ....
- ....
- ....
- ....
- ....
- ....
- ....

NOTES

....
....
....
....
....

THE PLAN FOR TODAY

DATE   /   /

TODAY'S GOAL

....
....
....

HIGH-IMPACT TASKS

....
....
....
....
....
....

TO DO'S

- ....
- ....
- ....
- ....
- ....
- ....
- ....

NOTES

....
....
....
....
....

THE WEEK AHEAD

WEEK BEGINNING   /   /

GOALS FOR THIS WEEK

....

....

....

MONDAY

....

TUESDAY

....

WEDNESDAY

....

THURSDAY

....

FRIDAY

....

SATURDAY

....

SUNDAY

....

THE PLAN FOR TODAY

DATE   /   /

TODAY'S GOAL

....
....
....

HIGH-IMPACT TASKS

....
....
....
....
....
....

TO DO'S

- ....
- ....
- ....
- ....
- ....
- ....
- ....

NOTES

....
....
....
....
....

THE PLAN FOR TODAY

TODAY'S GOAL

....
....
....

HIGH-IMPACT TASKS

....
....
....
....
....
....

TO DO'S

- ....
- ....
- ....
- ....
- ....
- ....
- ....

NOTES

....
....
....
....
....

THE PLAN FOR TODAY

DATE / /

TODAY'S GOAL

....

....

....

HIGH-IMPACT TASKS

....

....

....

....

....

....

TO DO'S

- ....
- ....
- ....
- ....
- ....
- ....
- ....

NOTES

....

....

....

....

....

THE PLAN FOR TODAY

DATE   /   /

TODAY'S GOAL

....
....
....

HIGH-IMPACT TASKS

....
....
....
....
....
....

TO DO'S

- [ ] ....
- [ ] ....
- [ ] ....
- [ ] ....
- [ ] ....
- [ ] ....
- [ ] ....

NOTES

....
....
....
....
....

DIAL DOWN THE DISTRACTIONS

Distractions come in many shapes and sizes but are most commonly digital these days. In today's business world, many people work in an open office setting, with all the attendant noise and movement associated with working in the midst of controlled chaos. Even in our homes, distractions abound and can interfere with the most basic chores or projects.

When you're working on something that requires focus, the best way to avoid being distracted by these digital interruptions is to simply shut them down.

Tips for avoiding distractions:

- Start by turning off or silencing computer and phone notifications.
- Set up a temporary autoreply on your e-mail to let others know you're unavailable and will respond later.
- Put a sign on your office door or cubicle that asks people not to interrupt you for a specified time period.
- Use earbuds or noise-canceling headphones as a signal to your coworkers that you're busy and focused.

Say "no" to inanimate time vampires. If your intention is to do just a "quick check" of Facebook or Instagram before starting your project, but you find yourself getting sucked into hours of scrolling, set a timer to remind yourself to get back to work. Or try an app to limit your time on social media. Two current ones are Offtime and Space, which allow you to monitor how much time you're spending online, let you set up controls for smartphone use, and give you incentives to unplug. Whatever your particular time vampire may be, human or otherwise, being proactive and having a ready response or an established coping mechanism to deal with it (or him or her) is the key to getting more done.

THE PLAN FOR TODAY

DATE   /   /

TODAY'S GOAL

....
....
....

HIGH-IMPACT TASKS

....
....
....
....
....
....

TO DO'S

- [ ] ....
- [ ] ....
- [ ] ....
- [ ] ....
- [ ] ....
- [ ] ....
- [ ] ....

NOTES

....
....
....
....
....

THE PLAN FOR TODAY

DATE   /   /

TODAY'S GOAL

....
....
....

HIGH-IMPACT TASKS

....
....
....
....
....
....

TO DO'S

- ....
- ....
- ....
- ....
- ....
- ....
- ....

NOTES

....
....
....
....
....

THE PLAN FOR TODAY

DATE / /

TODAY'S GOAL

....

....

....

HIGH-IMPACT TASKS

....

....

....

....

....

....

TO DO'S

- ....

- ....

- ....

- ....

- ....

- ....

- ....

NOTES

....

....

....

....

....

On average, it takes more than 2 months before a new behavior becomes automatic – 66 days to be exact.

—JAMES CLEAR

THE WEEK AHEAD

GOALS FOR THIS WEEK

....

....

....

MONDAY

....

TUESDAY

....

WEDNESDAY

....

THURSDAY

....

FRIDAY

....

SATURDAY

....

SUNDAY

....

THE PLAN FOR TODAY

TODAY'S GOAL

....
....
....

HIGH-IMPACT TASKS

....
....
....
....
....
....

TO DO'S

- ....
- ....
- ....
- ....
- ....
- ....
- ....

NOTES

....
....
....
....
....

THE PLAN FOR TODAY

DATE   /   /

TODAY'S GOAL

....

....

....

HIGH-IMPACT TASKS

....

....

....

....

....

....

TO DO'S

- [ ] ....
- [ ] ....
- [ ] ....
- [ ] ....
- [ ] ....
- [ ] ....
- [ ] ....

NOTES

....

....

....

....

....

THE PLAN FOR TODAY

TODAY'S GOAL

....
....
....

HIGH-IMPACT TASKS

....
....
....
....
....
....

TO DO'S

- ....
- ....
- ....
- ....
- ....
- ....
- ....

NOTES

....
....
....
....
....

THE PLAN FOR TODAY

TODAY'S GOAL

....
....
....

HIGH-IMPACT TASKS

....
....
....
....
....
....

TO DO'S

- ....
- ....
- ....
- ....
- ....
- ....
- ....

NOTES

....
....
....
....
....

"DONE" IS BETTER THAN "PERFECT"

Are you a perfectionist? Does everything have to be done to your exacting standards? If you can't do it perfectly, it's not worth doing, right? As a result, the project never gets finished, because it's never good enough—so why bother trying?

Stress builds as you can't find what you need, your frustration climbs, and you're still wasting time and money. As a reformed perfectionist, I have a mantra that I'd like you to repeat when you find yourself sinking into the mire of perfectionism: "Done is better than perfect."

Half-finished projects will not gain you more time or relieve your stress; they just cause you more stress, because having half-finished stuff hanging over your head makes you feel worse.

Increasing your productivity requires getting to the root of your perfectionism and asking tough questions. Is it a fear of failure? Have you tried and tried and never succeeded? Do you hold yourself to impossibly high standards? Are you trying to meet others' impossible standards? Some difficult self-analysis may be necessary to discover what exactly is getting in your way.

Reflect on how you feel when you must turn in a report that's not "perfect," or when you put off starting a project because you believe you will never be able to get it to look like the vision in your head. Dig down deep. Explore the feelings that got you to this point.

Perfectionism is almost always related in some way to fear: fear of failure, fear of not living up to others' expectations, fear that others' love and approval is conditional upon performance, fear of loss of control. When you identify what's getting in your way of letting go of perfection, you will come much closer to escaping from the stranglehold that perfectionism can have on your productivity growth.

THE PLAN FOR TODAY

DATE   /   /

TODAY'S GOAL

....
....
....

HIGH-IMPACT TASKS

....
....
....
....
....
....

TO DO'S

- ....
- ....
- ....
- ....
- ....
- ....
- ....

NOTES

....
....
....
....
....

THE PLAN FOR TODAY

DATE   /   /

TODAY'S GOAL

HIGH-IMPACT TASKS

TO DO'S

- [ ]
- [ ]
- [ ]
- [ ]
- [ ]
- [ ]
- [ ]

NOTES

THE PLAN FOR TODAY

TODAY'S GOAL

....
....
....

HIGH-IMPACT TASKS

....
....
....
....
....
....

TO DO'S

- ....
- ....
- ....
- ....
- ....
- ....
- ....

NOTES

....
....
....
....

Perfect is the enemy of good.

—VOLTAIRE

THIS MONTH IN REVIEW

1. Did I accomplish my goals for the month?

....
....
....
....
....
....
....
....

3. If my monthly, weekly, or daily goals were not met, what prevented this?

....
....
....
....
....
....
....

2. Did doing so get me closer to achieving a long-term goal?

....
....
....
....
....
....
....
....

4. How will I solve this problem next month?

....
....
....
....
....
....
....

NOTES

....
....
....
....
....
....
....
....
....
....
....
....
....
....
....
....
....
....
....
....
....
....
....
....
....
....
....
....
....
....

THIS MONTH IN FOCUS

GOALS FOR THIS MONTH

....

....

....

1	....	22	....
2	....	23	....
3	....	24	....
4	....	25	....
5	....	26	....
6	....	27	....
7	....	28	....
8	....	29	....
9	....	30	....
10	....	31	....
11	....		
12	....		
13	....		
14	....		
15	....		
16	....		
17	....		
18	....		
19	....		
20	....		
21	....		

MONTH

YEAR

NOTES AND REMINDERS

THE WEEK AHEAD

WEEK BEGINNING   /   /

GOALS FOR THIS WEEK

....

....

....

MONDAY

....

TUESDAY

....

WEDNESDAY

....

THURSDAY

....

FRIDAY

....

SATURDAY

....

SUNDAY

....

THE PLAN FOR TODAY

TODAY'S GOAL

....
....
....

HIGH-IMPACT TASKS

....
....
....
....
....
....

TO DO'S

- [ ] ....
- [ ] ....
- [ ] ....
- [ ] ....
- [ ] ....
- [ ] ....
- [ ] ....

NOTES

....
....
....
....
....

THE PLAN FOR TODAY

DATE   /   /

TODAY'S GOAL

....
....
....

HIGH-IMPACT TASKS

....
....
....
....
....
....

TO DO'S

- ....
- ....
- ....
- ....
- ....
- ....
- ....

NOTES

....
....
....
....
....

THE PLAN FOR TODAY

DATE   /   /

TODAY'S GOAL

....
....
....

HIGH-IMPACT TASKS

....
....
....
....
....
....

TO DO'S

☐ ....
☐ ....
☐ ....
☐ ....
☐ ....
☐ ....
☐ ....

NOTES

....
....
....
....
....

KNOW YOUR PRIME PRODUCTIVE TIME

What's your most productive time of the day? Several time management and productivity experts believe that early morning is the best time of the day to get difficult work done. Time and again, you read about highly successful people who rise at 4:00 a.m., work out, answer their e-mails, and write the great American novel, all before 9:00 a.m.!

If that's what works for you, go for it! However, there are many people for whom getting out of bed, getting dressed, and getting to work in one piece by 9:00 a.m. is a major accomplishment. Figuring out what time of day your brain is at its peak is a key factor in boosting your productivity. For some people, the early hours of the day are when they concentrate best and get their most difficult work done. Many others find that late afternoon, evening, or even late at night is the time when their brain really reaches its peak efficiency.

Studies have shown that fighting your natural biological tendencies can be difficult and often counterproductive (Black 2009; Breus 2009). The world is structured for success for those who are morning larks rather than night owls. When your most productive time is later in the day or even later at night, you can adjust your tasks to fit your most productive hours. Even if your job requires you to be in the office between 9:00 a.m. and 5:00 p.m., you can try to schedule tasks that aren't of significant impact, or are the least consequential, before lunch. Identify your most important work and plan to do it later in the afternoon, when your focus is better. When you identify your peak productivity time of the day or night, you can schedule the tasks that require deep brain work during that time and be more productive overall.

THE PLAN FOR TODAY

DATE   /   /

TODAY'S GOAL

....
....
....

HIGH-IMPACT TASKS

....
....
....
....
....
....

TO DO'S

- ....
- ....
- ....
- ....
- ....
- ....
- ....

NOTES

....
....
....
....
....

THE PLAN FOR TODAY

DATE   /   /

TODAY'S GOAL

....
....
....

HIGH-IMPACT TASKS

....
....
....
....
....
....

TO DO'S

- ....
- ....
- ....
- ....
- ....
- ....
- ....

NOTES

....
....
....
....
....

THE PLAN FOR TODAY

DATE / /

TODAY'S GOAL

....
....
....

HIGH-IMPACT TASKS

....
....
....
....
....
....

TO DO'S

- ....
- ....
- ....
- ....
- ....
- ....
- ....

NOTES

....
....
....
....
....

THE PLAN FOR TODAY

TODAY'S GOAL

....
....
....

HIGH-IMPACT TASKS

....
....
....
....
....
....

TO DO'S

- ....
- ....
- ....
- ....
- ....
- ....
- ....

NOTES

....
....
....
....
....

Suffice it to say that something automatic and extraordinary happens in your mind when you create and focus on a clear picture of what you want.

—DAVID ALLEN

THE WEEK AHEAD

GOALS FOR THIS WEEK

....

....

....

MONDAY

....

TUESDAY

....

WEDNESDAY

....

THURSDAY

....

FRIDAY

....

SATURDAY

....

SUNDAY

....

THE PLAN FOR TODAY

DATE   /   /

TODAY'S GOAL

....

....

....

HIGH-IMPACT TASKS

....

....

....

....

....

....

TO DO'S

- ....
- ....
- ....
- ....
- ....
- ....
- ....

NOTES

....

....

....

....

....

THE PLAN FOR TODAY

TODAY'S GOAL

....
....
....

HIGH-IMPACT TASKS

....
....
....
....
....
....

TO DO'S

☐ ....
☐ ....
☐ ....
☐ ....
☐ ....
☐ ....
☐ ....

NOTES

....
....
....
....
....

THE PLAN FOR TODAY

TODAY'S GOAL

....

....

....

HIGH-IMPACT TASKS

....

....

....

....

....

....

TO DO'S

- ☐ ....
- ☐ ....
- ☐ ....
- ☐ ....
- ☐ ....
- ☐ ....
- ☐ ....

NOTES

....

....

....

....

....

THE PLAN FOR TODAY

TODAY'S GOAL

....

....

....

HIGH-IMPACT TASKS

....

....

....

....

....

....

TO DO'S

- ....
- ....
- ....
- ....
- ....
- ....
- ....

NOTES

....

....

....

....

....

THE FINE ART OF DELEGATING

"If I want it done right, I have to do it myself." Does this sound familiar?

Often, our productivity is impeded by the fact that we simply have too much to do. One reason for this may be our reluctance to delegate tasks. This can be another aspect of perfectionism, where your standards are simply so high that no one could meet them. If you've reached the point of feeling like you're the one who must do it all, you need to accept the fact that it's time to let things go.

If your teenager can expertly manipulate a smartphone, she or he can empty the dishwasher. Your assistant could take on that spreadsheet you've been laboring over. It may not be formatted exactly the way you would do it, but it would be done, off your plate, and containing the information you need. Train others to do the work, or create written step-by-step training materials. This will allow other people to continue taking on tasks and getting them off your plate, and doing the tasks the way you want them done.

When you let go and let others help, you may find capabilities and talents in those people that you didn't know they had. And even if the tasks may not be done to your exacting standards, it may be time to recognize that getting things done is the main goal here and that delegating frees up your time to pursue larger goals. Try releasing just a few small things at a time, and take a little extra time to teach or show the responsible person how you would like the task done. With regular practice, you will find you'll be able to delegate larger tasks more freely.

THE PLAN FOR TODAY

DATE   /   /

TODAY'S GOAL

....
....
....

HIGH-IMPACT TASKS

....
....
....
....
....
....

TO DO'S

- ....
- ....
- ....
- ....
- ....
- ....
- ....

NOTES

....
....
....
....
....

THE PLAN FOR TODAY

DATE   /   /

TODAY'S GOAL

....
....
....

HIGH-IMPACT TASKS

....
....
....
....
....
....

TO DO'S

- ....
- ....
- ....
- ....
- ....
- ....
- ....

NOTES

....
....
....
....

THE PLAN FOR TODAY

DATE / /

TODAY'S GOAL

....

....

....

HIGH-IMPACT TASKS

....

....

....

....

....

....

TO DO'S

- ....
- ....
- ....
- ....
- ....
- ....
- ....

NOTES

....

....

....

....

....

THE WEEK AHEAD

WEEK BEGINNING / /

GOALS FOR THIS WEEK

....

....

....

MONDAY

....

TUESDAY

....

WEDNESDAY

....

THURSDAY

....

FRIDAY

....

SATURDAY

....

SUNDAY

....

THE PLAN FOR TODAY

DATE   /   /

TODAY'S GOAL

....
....
....

HIGH-IMPACT TASKS

....
....
....
....
....
....

TO DO'S

- [ ] ....
- [ ] ....
- [ ] ....
- [ ] ....
- [ ] ....
- [ ] ....
- [ ] ....

NOTES

....
....
....
....
....

THE PLAN FOR TODAY

DATE / /

TODAY'S GOAL

....
....
....

HIGH-IMPACT TASKS

....
....
....
....
....
....

TO DO'S

- ....
- ....
- ....
- ....
- ....
- ....
- ....

NOTES

....
....
....
....
....

THE PLAN FOR TODAY

TODAY'S GOAL

....
....
....

HIGH-IMPACT TASKS

....
....
....
....
....
....

TO DO'S

- ....
- ....
- ....
- ....
- ....
- ....
- ....

NOTES

....
....
....
....
....

GATHER YOUR THOUGHTS
AND YOUR MATERIALS

Getting started on a task or project may be the most difficult part of the job. After breaking projects down into tasks, the next step is to make sure you have within easy reach everything you need to accomplish each task. Gather your materials ahead of time so you don't have to break your focus and waste time searching for things you need to move forward.

If you're working on a home improvement project, have one of your tasks be to make a list of all the necessary tools and supplies, then hit the hardware store ahead of time to get them. This ensures you can get your project done in a timely fashion, without multiple breaks either to search for what you need or to go out and buy it.

Let's say your designated project is to do your taxes. At a minimum, you will need the following:

1. A tax preparation program/software or to choose a person or service to do the taxes for you.
2. Receipts and backup documents for any deductions you claim.
3. Income documents such as W-2 forms, 1099 forms, or K-1 forms for investment income.
4. A credit card to pay for the online program or a check to pay for the physical person (such as a CPA) or service (like H&R Block).
5. Your bank account information for getting your refund after e-filing.

Preparation is the key to success for any endeavor. It will also enable you to enter more quickly into a "flow state," a term coined by psychologist Mihaly Csikszentmihalyi. Being in the flow state means being fully mentally and physically involved in any task with complete focus and enjoyment. Getting "into flow" is what allows you to accomplish concentrated brain work more quickly, more efficiently, and more productively.

THE PLAN FOR TODAY

DATE / /

TODAY'S GOAL

....
....
....

HIGH-IMPACT TASKS

....
....
....
....
....
....

TO DO'S

- ....
- ....
- ....
- ....
- ....
- ....
- ....

NOTES

....
....
....
....
....

THE PLAN FOR TODAY

DATE / /

TODAY'S GOAL

....
....
....

HIGH-IMPACT TASKS

....
....
....
....
....
....

TO DO'S

- ....
- ....
- ....
- ....
- ....
- ....
- ....

NOTES

....
....
....
....
....

THE PLAN FOR TODAY

DATE / /

TODAY'S GOAL

....
....
....

HIGH-IMPACT TASKS

....
....
....
....
....
....

TO DO'S

- ....
- ....
- ....
- ....
- ....
- ....
- ....

NOTES

....
....
....
....
....

THE PLAN FOR TODAY

DATE / /

TODAY'S GOAL

....

....

....

HIGH-IMPACT TASKS

....

....

....

....

....

....

TO DO'S

- ....
- ....
- ....
- ....
- ....
- ....
- ....

NOTES

....

....

....

....

....

THE WEEK AHEAD

WEEK BEGINNING   /   /

GOALS FOR THIS WEEK

....

....

....

MONDAY

....

TUESDAY

....

WEDNESDAY

....

THURSDAY

....

FRIDAY

....

SATURDAY

....

SUNDAY

....

THE PLAN FOR TODAY

DATE   /   /

TODAY'S GOAL

....
....
....

HIGH-IMPACT TASKS

....
....
....
....
....
....

TO DO'S

- ....
- ....
- ....
- ....
- ....
- ....
- ....

NOTES

....
....
....
....
....

THE PLAN FOR TODAY

DATE   /   /

TODAY'S GOAL

....
....
....

HIGH-IMPACT TASKS

....
....
....
....
....
....

TO DO'S

- [ ] ....
- [ ] ....
- [ ] ....
- [ ] ....
- [ ] ....
- [ ] ....
- [ ] ....

NOTES

....
....
....
....
....

THE PLAN FOR TODAY

DATE / /

TODAY'S GOAL

....
....
....

HIGH-IMPACT TASKS

....
....
....
....
....
....

TO DO'S

- ....
- ....
- ....
- ....
- ....
- ....
- ....

NOTES

....
....
....
....
....

THE PLAN FOR TODAY

DATE   /   /

TODAY'S GOAL

....
....
....

HIGH-IMPACT TASKS

....
....
....
....
....
....

TO DO'S

- [ ] ....
- [ ] ....
- [ ] ....
- [ ] ....
- [ ] ....
- [ ] ....
- [ ] ....

NOTES

....
....
....
....
....

BUILDING GOOD HABITS, BREAKING BAD ONES

Improving your productivity requires changing the way you do things. Making the conscious decision to do things differently is the first step toward getting more done in less time with less stress. In order to accomplish this, it's necessary to break old habits and build new ones. Fighting your perfectionist tendencies, allowing others to take on tasks, and taking the time to plan out each month, week, and day all require establishing new habits.

The first step is to decide you're ready for change. Without that commitment, it will be too easy to fall back into your old way of doing things. Start small—don't try to change everything at once. Choose one habit at a time to change, such as blocking your access to social media at certain times or checking e-mails only two or three times a day instead of constantly. Commit to your new habit and create reminders for it. Have a sticky note nearby with encouraging words or set a calendar reminder for when it's time to unplug.

Remember, it takes about 21 days for something to become a habit, which is defined as "a regular tendency or practice." So, don't be too hard on yourself when you don't immediately remember to change something on days 2, 5, or even 17! It can take up to 30 repetitions of a new habit before it becomes ingrained. When you fail initially (and you will), don't give up. Forgive yourself, put the failure behind you, and start again.

Once you feel comfortable with your new habit, choose another one to implement.

The key is persistence and patience. It's impossible to get good at something without regular practice. Use this planner every single day to form these new, more productive habits that will help you reach your goals.

THE PLAN FOR TODAY

DATE   /   /

TODAY'S GOAL

....
....
....

HIGH-IMPACT TASKS

....
....
....
....
....
....

TO DO'S

- ....
- ....
- ....
- ....
- ....
- ....
- ....

NOTES

....
....
....
....

THE PLAN FOR TODAY

DATE   /   /

TODAY'S GOAL

....
....
....

HIGH-IMPACT TASKS

....
....
....
....
....
....

TO DO'S

- ....
- ....
- ....
- ....
- ....
- ....
- ....

NOTES

....
....
....
....
....

THE PLAN FOR TODAY

DATE / /

TODAY'S GOAL

....
....
....

HIGH-IMPACT TASKS

....
....
....
....
....
....

TO DO'S

- ....
- ....
- ....
- ....
- ....
- ....
- ....

NOTES

....
....
....
....

The only motivational advice anyone has ever needed: You don't have to feel like getting something done in order to actually get it done.

—MELISSA DAHL

THE WEEK AHEAD

GOALS FOR THIS WEEK

....

....

....

MONDAY

....

TUESDAY

....

WEDNESDAY

....

THURSDAY

....

FRIDAY

....

SATURDAY

....

SUNDAY

....

THE PLAN FOR TODAY

DATE   /   /

TODAY'S GOAL

....
....
....

HIGH-IMPACT TASKS

....
....
....
....
....
....

TO DO'S

- ....
- ....
- ....
- ....
- ....
- ....
- ....

NOTES

....
....
....
....
....

THE PLAN FOR TODAY

DATE   /   /

TODAY'S GOAL

....
....
....

HIGH-IMPACT TASKS

....
....
....
....
....
....

TO DO'S

- ....
- ....
- ....
- ....
- ....
- ....
- ....

NOTES

....
....
....
....
....

THE PLAN FOR TODAY

TODAY'S GOAL

....
....
....

HIGH-IMPACT TASKS

....
....
....
....
....
....

TO DO'S

- [ ] ....
- [ ] ....
- [ ] ....
- [ ] ....
- [ ] ....
- [ ] ....
- [ ] ....

NOTES

....
....
....
....
....

PLANNERS AREN'T MAGIC WANDS

As a productivity consultant, I see clients fall into the same traps time and again. One of the biggest errors in their thinking is that there is a magic tool out there that will automatically make them manage their time more efficiently and help them get more done. They buy planner after planner, download app after app, try each new thing for a few days, and when it doesn't immediately change their life, they abandon it.

This planner is a terrific tool to get you started on the path to improved productivity, but it's not a *magic* planner. It's not a sorcerer who waves his magic wand and makes all of the dirty dishes, piles of clothes, brooms, and sponges instantaneously spring into action and do the cleaning themselves. Just as there is no magic pill for weight loss, there is no magic plan for productivity. Being more productive and practicing effective time management is an ongoing lifestyle change.

What you are missing when you make grand efforts to search out the "best" productivity tool is that almost any good tool would work. It is necessary to choose one, then use it consistently, conscientiously, and thoroughly for it to be effective. It's not about the "stuff"—the tools, apps, calendar reminders, and so on. It's about making the conscious decision to change and then following through with pushing aside your old habits and choosing to align yourself with new ones.

By making a commitment to change and then using this planner and following the steps outlined for a solid 90 days, each day, every day, you are making that change. Here is your one tool—coupled with your decision to do things differently—that will make the difference in your life.

THE PLAN FOR TODAY

DATE / /

TODAY'S GOAL

....

....

....

HIGH-IMPACT TASKS

....

....

....

....

....

....

TO DO'S

- ....
- ....
- ....
- ....
- ....
- ....
- ....

NOTES

....

....

....

....

....

THE PLAN FOR TODAY

DATE   /   /

TODAY'S GOAL

....
....
....

HIGH-IMPACT TASKS

....
....
....
....
....
....

TO DO'S

- ....
- ....
- ....
- ....
- ....
- ....
- ....

NOTES

....
....
....
....
....

THE PLAN FOR TODAY

DATE   /   /

TODAY'S GOAL

....
....
....

HIGH-IMPACT TASKS

....
....
....
....
....
....

TO DO'S

- [ ] ....
- [ ] ....
- [ ] ....
- [ ] ....
- [ ] ....
- [ ] ....
- [ ] ....

NOTES

....
....
....
....
....

THE PLAN FOR TODAY

DATE / /

TODAY'S GOAL

....
....
....

HIGH-IMPACT TASKS

....
....
....
....
....
....

TO DO'S

- ....
- ....
- ....
- ....
- ....
- ....
- ....

NOTES

....
....
....
....
....

The secret of getting ahead is getting started. The secret of getting started is breaking your complex overwhelming tasks into small, manageable tasks, and then starting on the first one.

—MARK TWAIN

THIS MONTH IN REVIEW

1. Did I accomplish my goals for the month?

....
....
....
....
....
....
....
....

3. If my monthly, weekly, or daily goals were not met, what prevented this?

....
....
....
....
....
....
....

2. Did doing so get me closer to achieving a long-term goal?

....
....
....
....
....
....
....
....

4. How will I solve this problem next month?

....
....
....
....
....
....
....

MONTH

YEAR

NOTES

WHERE TO GO FROM HERE

Congratulations! You've reached the end of your 90-day journey with this planner. Three months ago, you made the decision to become more productive and take control of your time. You made a commitment to plan out your goals and tasks on a daily, weekly, and monthly basis. Often, a journey such as this requires deep personal introspection as you realize how you've been spending your time in the past.

I hope you've seen that defining your goals, making them S.M.A.R.T., and planning each day with those goals in mind help you better manage your time and get stuff done. Now you know that spending a small amount of time planning gains you a great deal of time later.

Now that you've established some good time management habits, take stock of what you found most helpful. Ask yourself a few questions:

- What, if anything, about this planner helped you learn to implement better habits?
- Were you able to increase your productivity as you had hoped?

  - If so, how do you plan to maintain your new level of productivity? Do you feel prepared to continue?
  - If not, what got in your way?

- Were you able to use this planner to its fullest extent?
- Did using this planner help you more specifically define your goals and the tasks you needed to do to achieve those goals?
- Did you find that spending a small amount of time planning out your days in advance helped you achieve your larger goals?
- Are you more conscious of the value of your time and what you spend your time doing?
- Have you learned to delegate tasks and reschedule the ones you cannot complete at a given moment?
- How has the experience of learning to break projects down into individual tasks helped you complete projects? Will you continue to work on projects this way?

As you move on, I hope you find that the information and structure provided here has helped you define more clearly how you're spending your time, as well as shown you how to manage your time more effectively and gain more from each day.

My goal in putting together this planner was for you to find yourself getting more done with every moment of each day, and having more time for the things that bring you joy. My hope is that whatever you're longing for—spending more time with your family, taking better care of yourself with exercise and nutrition, getting ahead in your job, or taking that long-awaited vacation—will be within your grasp as you benefit from more time in your life.

RESOURCES

ORGANIZATIONS:

ICD. Institute for Challenging Disorganization. challengingdisorganization.org.

NAPO. National Association of Productivity and Organizing Professionals. napo.net.

APPS:

Offtime. https://offtime.app/.

Space. https://findyourphonelifebalance.com/.

BOOKS:

Allen, David. *Getting Things Done: The Art of Stress-Free Productivity*. New York: Penguin Group, 2001.

Carter, Christine. *The Sweet Spot: How to Accomplish More By Doing Less*. New York: Ballantine Books, 2015.

Duhigg, Charles. *Smarter, Faster, Better: The Secrets of Being Productive in Life and Business*. New York: Random House, 2017.

Kogon, Kory, Adam Merrill, and Leena Rinne. *The Five Choices: The Path to Extraordinary Productivity*. New York: Simon & Schuster, Inc., 2015.

Morgenstern, Julie. *Time Management from the Inside Out*. New York: Henry Holt and Company, 2004.

Tracy, Brian. *Eat That Frog: 21 Great Ways to Stop Procrastinating and Get More Done in Less Time*. San Francisco: Berrett-Koehler Publishers, Inc., 2017.

REFERENCES

Allen, David. *Getting Things Done: The Art of Stress-Free Productivity.* New York: Penguin Group, 2001.

American Psychological Association. "Multitasking: Switching Costs." (March 20, 2006). https://www.apa.org/research/action/multitask.

Benson, Etienne. "The Many Faces of Perfectionism." *American Psychological Association* 34, no. 10 (November 2003): 18. https://www.apa.org/monitor/nov03/manyfaces.html.

Black, Rosemary. "Early to Rise, Quick to Succeed? Not for Everyone, Studies Find." *Daily News* (November 30, 2009). https://www.nydailynews.com/life-style/early-rise-quick-succeed-not-studies-find-article-1.436466.

Breus, Michael, PhD. "The Lark vs. the Owl: Don't Mess with Mother Nature." *Psychology Today* (December 16, 2009). https://www.psychologytoday.com/us/blog/sleep-newzzz/200912/the-lark-vs-the-owl-don-t-mess-mother-nature.

Carter, Christine. *The Sweet Spot: How to Find Your Groove at Home and Work.* New York: Ballantine Books, 2015.

Carter, Sherrie Bourg. "Why Mess Causes Stress: 8 Reasons, 8 Remedies." *Psychology Today* (March 14, 2012). https://www.psychologytoday.com/us/blog/high-octane-women/201203/why-mess-causes-stress-8-reasons-8-remedies.

Clear, James. "How Long Does It Actually Take to Form a New Habit? (Backed by Science)." https://jamesclear.com/new-habit.

Csikszentmihalyi, Mihaly. *Flow: The Classic Work on How to Achieve Happiness.* London: Ebury Press, 2002.

Davidson, Jeff. "What to Do When Your Boss Keeps Interrupting You." Breathingspace.com (blog) (2012). https://breathingspace.com/what-to-do-when-your-boss-keeps-interrupting-you/.

Doland, Erin. "Scientists Find Physical Clutter Negatively Affects Your Ability to Focus, Process Information." Unclutterer.com (blog) (March 29, 2011). https://unclutterer.com/2011/03/29/scientists-find-physical-clutter-negatively-affects-your-ability-to-focus-process-information/.

Duhigg, Charles. *Smarter, Faster, Better: The Secrets of Being Productive in Life and Business.* New York: Random House, 2016.

Forbes Coaches Council. "15 Proven Strategies for Building and Dropping Habits." *Forbes* (June 22, 2018). https://www.forbes.com/sites /forbescoachescouncil/2018/06/22/15-proven-strategies-for-building -and-dropping-habits/#6a6db2675872.

Gorlick, Adam. "Media Multitaskers Pay Mental Price, Stanford Study Shows." *Stanford News* (August 24, 2009). https://news.stanford.edu /2009/08/24/multitask-research-study-082409/.

Gregoire, Carolyn. "14 Signs Your Perfectionism Has Gotten Out of Control." *Huffington Post* (December 7, 2017). https://www.huffpost.com /entry/why-perfectionism-is-ruin_n_4212069.

Kogon, Kory, Adam, Merrill, and Leena Rinne. *The Five Choices: The Path to Extraordinary Productivity.* New York: Simon & Schuster, Inc., 2015.

McMains, Stephanie, and Sabine Kastner. "Interactions of Top-Down and Bottom-Up Mechanisms in Human Visual Cortex." *Journal of Neuroscience* 31, no. 2 (January 12, 2011): 587–597. doi:10.1523/JNEUROSCI.3766-10.2011.

Morgenstern, Julie. *Time Management from the Inside Out.* New York: St. Martin's Press, 2004.

Tracy, Brian. *Time Power: A Proven System for Getting More Done in Less Time Than You Ever Thought Possible.* New York: AMACOM, 2007.

———*Eat That Frog!: 21 Great Ways to Stop Procrastinating and Get More Done in Less Time.* San Francisco: Berrett-Koehler Publishers, Inc., 2017.

University of Illinois at Urbana-Champaign. "Brief Diversions Vastly Improve Focus, Researchers Find." *ScienceDaily* (February 8, 2011). Accessed May 23, 2019. https://www.sciencedaily.com/releases/2011/02/110208131529.htm.

Whitbourne, Susan Krauss, PhD. "A New Way to Understand Procrastination." *Psychology Today* (January 9, 2018). https://www.psychologytoday.com /us/blog/fulfillment-any-age/201801/new-way-understand-procrastination.

ACKNOWLEDGMENTS

To Hannah R. Goodman of writerwomyn.com: Without your encouragement and expert guidance, I would never have been confident enough to put pen to paper. You helped me believe I could.

To Robert T. Griffith, husband extraordinaire: For your patience, understanding, support, and endless love over the past 41 years. Marrying you was the single best decision of my life.

ABOUT THE AUTHOR

Lisa S. Griffith is a Certified Professional Organizer®, productivity consultant, and speaker who began her career as a teacher, director, and administrator of performing arts in schools, churches, and community organizations. In 2008, she decided to put her more than 30 years of teaching, organizational, and administrative skills to work and established her business, The Organized Way. Her specialties are business office organizing and time management coaching, and she particularly enjoys working with entrepreneurs and business owners who are looking to get a new business off the ground or to establish organizational processes and systems for existing businesses.

Lisa offers one-on-one consulting both on-site and in virtual settings, workshops on organizing and productivity topics, and seminars for groups. In addition to her client work, she regularly speaks to groups of all sizes for professional, educational, and community organizations. Lisa holds a certificate in time management and productivity from the Institute for Challenging Disorganization, is a member of the National Association of Productivity and Organizing Professionals (NAPO), and is active in her local NAPO-New England chapter.